Exploring
The Seven Aspects
of
GOD

GOD Cards Companion Guide

Inspired by the writings of Emmet Fox

Zia Eubanks

Exploring the Seven Aspects of God

GOD Cards Companion Guide

Inspired by the writings of Emmet Fox

Copyright © 2020 Zia Eubanks

ISBN: 978-0-9992133-3-9

Dedication

This book is dedicated to my Gemini Twin Flame, Larry Peterson. The love, support, and encouragement he has bathed me in during this process is something I have never experienced before. I am filled with gratitude for his presence in my life. He has reminded me to honor my creative gifts and understand that when I create I am expressing my God essence.

Preface

The word GOD means something different to everyone. It can be a word that comforts, soothes and calms many people. But, for others it evokes memories of a childhood father figure that was punitive and judgmental.

As I transitioned through my own spiritual journey I had an issue with the word and the understanding of God. The God of my childhood reminded me of Santa Claus - all knowing, always watching and keeping a detailed record of when I was good and when I was bad. That God had the power to decide if I was going to Heaven or Hell. It was a scary concept as a child. As I matured and moved into adulthood, my concepts changed and I knew that I had to elevate my understanding and relationship with this source of power in my life. I decided that I had to eliminate the gender identification. God wasn't an old man with a beard, in white robes ,floating in the sky, watching over me. I switched to a more cosmic concept and began to refer to that power as "Source" or "Universe". It felt more real to me.

As my consciousness expanded so did my concept of God. The terms Source and Universe were very inclusive and related to my adult understanding of God, but lacked a sense of intimacy. This God of my understanding, that I called Universe, was an energy that ran through all things. It was the spirit that animated Life. It was a power that charged all of existence. Universe and Source were good words but didn't seem big enough to describe that power I had come to know. I knew I wanted to embrace the word "God" as my own again. But, I needed to really define it for myself.

As the mystery of coincidence works, I came across a little booklet by Emmet Fox. He was a New Thought spiritual teacher born in 1886, and taught through the depression and on into his death in 1951. It was a short little book called "The Golden Key". *The concept in the book was to look at problems or situations in your life through the concept of God. Instead of focusing on the issue or problem, focus on the aspects of God. He referred to another of his booklets named,* "The Seven Main Aspects of God" *as a resource. I decided to order it. When the booklet came, it was small and very short. I thought how could this little booklet give me a new understanding of God? I read it through in one sitting. Afterwards, I sat in my reading chair and contemplated what I had read. I read it again. I had never read anything about God that had touched me so deeply as this little booklet.*

It was nearing the end of the year, and every year I pick a word to be my focus word for the year. After reading the booklet and contemplating what I had read, I decided to choose GOD for my word for 2019, and I had decided to use Fox's little booklet "The Seven Main Aspects of God" to be my guide.

So in January I began. My goal was to fully understand my personal definition of God by the end of the year. I wanted to be able to say the word "God" and feel it in my heart and soul and know what it meant to me. A big challenge , I know.

Since my creativity is at the center of my life experience, I decided to study the booklet and dive into the concepts. I would mediate, read one of the aspects and then write about what it meant to me. As time progressed, I decided that I would break down each of the seven aspects and study them individually. The idea of Meditation/Inspiration cards sparked, and I began the process of making a deck of God Cards. I decided to create seven cards for each of the seven aspects. And one card as a "treatment" or prayer card. Each card that I created would help me to delve deeper into an understanding of an aspect of God.

This book and my God Card deck is a result of that process. It was a year in the making —the gift of the year. This process has aligned me with a rich and deep, heart felt concept and connection with the word God. When I say, "God" now, I feel it, I understand it and I own it. God is no longer some old man judging me, or some concept from my childhood faith. God is now the power and force that pulses through my body and brings me LIFE. God is omnipotent and omnipresent. God is Love!

The God I defined for myself is not related to any religion or faith. It is not gender identified. God IS everywhere, in everything and is the life force that animates all of existence. It is mysterious, yet ordered. And, of course, It is uniquely understood by everyone. Not one of us has the same experience of God. This book and my God Cards are my interpretation based on my study of Emmet Fox, plus the years of my own spiritual journey. Use them as it resonates with you.

This book is meant to stand alone, or be used as a companion to the God Cards Mediation/ Inspiration Deck. It is not meant to be read cover to cover, although you can. The concept is to use it as a mediation or inspirational prompt. Pick a page at random and read the message. Use it for further contemplation or for a boost of inspiration for the day. Feel free to use it anyway you choose!

My gratitude to Emmet Fox for his courage and insight to be true to his heart and beliefs in a time of conformity and fear. His words have taught me, what ancient wisdom continues to teach, God is not connected to a church or religion. God IS our connection to Life. We each have our own unique relationship to its power, exactly the way it should be! May this book help you in clarifying yours.

In the Spirit of Love,

Zia

Introduction

How To Use This Book

Meditation/Contemplation
Pick a card, read it, think about it and then meditate or contemplate the concept. Reflect on your life and how the card may have particular meaning to you.
You can also journal after meditation to further understand how it relates to you and your situation.

Have a Question?
If you are struggling with a situation or have some
issue that needs resolution, flip through the book

while thinking of your issue, and then pick one page to read. Read it over a couple of times and sense how it relates.

Choose more cards, in the same fashion, to get more information. Limit it to three to five cards. More than that will cloud the process.

Treatment Cards

When you identify an area (aspect) where you desire a shift in consciousness, use the treatment card as a prayer. Repeat it as often as you need, until your feel some shift. If you choose a Treatment Card during mediation or exploring an issue, take that as a sign that this is an aspect that needs your attention in a deeper manner.

Most of all, enjoy and use your intuition as your guide. Each and everyone of us has a "sixth" sense of some type, it is built into us. Use the cards as a way of tapping into that innate wisdom. They are a tool for you to awaken to the Truth of your unique expression. So many people are looking for ways to connect with their "purpose". Working with these cards can help you to better understand yourself and your divine design.

There is no right way,
there is only your way.

Let your exploration begin . .
.

Aspect One

God is

LIFE

LIFE   1

"Where GOD is,
there LIFE is."

~ Emmet Fox

LIFE 1

Life is existence or "being."

If you are human "being," then you are
God expressed as you!
The living presence.
Without it you have no life.
Life is your human
experience of God.

There is no separation.

LIFE 2,

"Joy is one of the highest expressions of God is Life."

— Emmet Fox

LIFE 2

Joy happens when you recognize
your own divinity.
(You are an expression of God
by the very means of your Life.)
Joy expands!

Sorrow is separation from Source.
(Not recognizing your life
is God expressed as you.)
Sorrow contracts.

The body always expresses
the thought; and the thought
of LIFE heals and inspires,
where as thoughts of fear and
death contract and destroy.

Emmet Fox

LIFE 3

Connecting to the aspect of God is Life
starts a chain reaction.
The more a person understands that
Life is the spark of good,
wholeness and health
the more Life will grow.

What God is, we are.
It is part of our essence of being.
The more we own it and live it,
the more joy and health we experience
in our everyday life.
Treat for Life!
Begin expanding self love,
health and joy!

LIFE 4

"When a person says, 'I CAN,' you always notice an expansive and forward movement, but when they say, 'I CAN'T,' there is retraction."

~ Emmet Fox

LIFE 4

"I CAN" opens up the possibilities.
It is expression of Life.
The words tell the truth of life.
Having life, being alive is God in
expression.
Saying, "I CAN" is knowing that what God
is,
you are. Anything is possible.

Aligning your "I CAN" with divine
principals automatically guarantees
demonstration (aka manifestation).

This is monumental, yet simple.
It is a mindset change.
Accepting God is Life will transform you!

LIFE

5

"When you are sick you are only partly alive. When you are tired or depressed or discouraged, you are only partly alive. Few people express God in an adequate way because they lack the sense of Life."

Emmet Fox

LIFE 5

Drench yourself with Love.

That is how to treat for Life.

Own and accept the Truth of your
beingness — what God is, I am.

When you hold yourself in the "I am"
consciousness and flood yourself
with love, then life is that of
joy and celebration.

"Joy and happiness always have an expansive effect, just as fear has a contracting and paralyzing effect."

Emmet Fox

LIFE 6

When you recognize God is Life,
you expand.

You see and feel the possibilities of
life. Just waking up, being alive, is
Spirit Incarnate!

That is something to celebrate and
feel joyful about!

Celebrate Life!

LIFE 7

"God is not just living, nor
does God give life, but
God is Life."

Emmet Fox

LIFE 7

God is Life.

There is no life without the mysterious
force of energy that we agree to call
God.
We are a unique expression of that
energy
having a physical experience.
Eventually the body will cease to exist,
but the energy within is eternal.

All the more reason to life fully!
At this moment you are alive and
God is why!

Great for LIFE

When your energy is low, or you have forgotten that every breath you take is a confirmation of life.

When you feel like things are "happening" to you or life is unfair.

When you get sucked into the drama and pettiness of the world.

When you are sick, tired, depressed, sad, or lonely.

OR, if life is good and you want to show your gratitude and super charge your life energy!

LIFE Treatment

There is one Source and that Source is everywhere, in all things.

I am an expression of the one and the oneness gives me Life!

Life is a gift. It is breath, it is emotions, it is experiencing form in the world of the senses. It is the Joy of Being.

I am filled with awe and gratitude for this holy gift. I hold it with respect and reverence and live Life fully!

Knowing this is true I let go and allow it to flow through me.

Aspect Two

God is

TRUTH

"God is not truthful but TRUTH
itself, and where ever there is
Truth, there is God."

~ Emmet Fox

ᏫᎡᏌᎢᎯ 1

You know it when you hear it or feel
It, real Truth.

It resonates on a deep level.
You don't have to question it,
you just know.

That is "God is Truth".
When it resonates that strongly
it is touching Divinity.

TRUTH 2

"As soon as we touch God, who is the absolute, relative things disappear."

~ Emmet Fox

CRUTH 2

To know the Truth about any
condition heals it.
No need to dissect it, analyze it, or
re-live it.

To know the Truth, on a spiritual
level is the understanding
of the perfect
order of Divinity.

Connecting with your own personal
Truth is the greatest healer.

TRUTH   3

"...wherever there is Truth,
there is God."

~ Emmet Fox

ᏒᏒᏌᏟᏂ 3

When you see things that are not truth
as real it
obscures the reality.

However, when we connect with
God (is Truth), that which is not truth
will fade away.

It is a shift in consciousness.
Things that once seemed important or
worrisome
vanish. It is perspective, awakening,
and acknowledging Truth!

TRUTH 4

"Realizing God is Truth will save you hours of research in any field. You will be led to the right book or the right place or the right person without loss of time or the necessary information will come to you in some other way."

~ Emmet Fox

CRUCH 4

You know Truth when you experience it.

Recognizing Truth and realizing the
Divine power it contains is like magic.

It can heal any situation, relieve stress
and confusion, and open up possibilities
previously unknown.
Information appears, people show up,
situations arise that lead you to exactly
what you need.

Sometimes Truth is hard to see,
and even harder to face,
but it is a sure connection to
spiritual unfoldment.

TRUTH 5

> "To know the Truth about any condition heals it. Truth is the great healer."
>
> Emmet Fox

TRUTH 5

Truth.

Truth is the knowing of God that
exists within.
It is a deep and powerful
understanding that resonates in a
place no one can touch.

When you connect with this internal
Truth you connect with
the Source of Life.

There is a freedom that engulfs you.
It can't be denied.

TRUTH 6

"... spend a few minutes realizing Divine Truth and if there is anything you need to know it will come out."

~ Emmet Fox

CRUCH 6

Divine Truth is the truth you feel within
on a level so deep it can't be ignored
or rebuffed.

Sometimes we get disconnected or
distracted from that inner Truth.

Take time to meditate and reconnect
with this inner knowing
at the core of your being.

It is always there for you,
available in the silence.
Ready to re-awaken and remind
you of who you truly are.

TRUTH 7

> ". . . . God is absolute Truth
> at all times and in all
> circumstances."
>
> ~ Emmet Fox

CRUCH 7

The Truth lies beyond the duality
of our human existence.

Truth, Divine Truth,
isn't about good or bad, right or wrong.
It is deep knowing that is felt in the
Soul.
It is always there, living,
breathing, and "being."

Don't get lost in analysis.
Surrender to it.
Allow it to guide you.

Treat for TRUTH

When you are confused about a
decision, or are involved in a
situation that has you perplexed,
treat for Truth.

If you are stuck in the duality of the
material world and feel like you are
choosing based on external factors,
treat for Truth.

Get silent, meditate and pray.

Once you connect with your Truth
you will know exactly what to do.

TRUTH Treatment

God is. I am.

There is a Truth within me that guides and inspires me. Today I open myself to that Divine Truth, and bask in its light. I know that this Truth is my foundation.

It is with deep gratitude that I accept this understanding and rejoice in awareness that it is mine.

And so it it.

Aspect Three

God is

LOVE

LOVE

I

"Where there is fear there cannot be love. The best way to rid yourself of fear is to realize Divine Love."

~ Emmet Fox

LOVE 1

Divine Love comes from the inside out,
not the reverse.
It is the connection that flows in all of life.
(God is Life)

Open your heart.

Fear creates a state of being that blocks love.
The world is filled with fear and manipulation.
You can choose it, or you can realize
God is Love and surrender
into the Truth of who you are.

Embrace LOVE!

LOVE

2

"Practice Love everyday and watch your thought, and watch your tongue, and watch your deed, that nothing contrary to Love finds expression there."

Emmet Fox

LOVE 2

Elevate your vibration.
Divine Love vibrates at the highest frequency
and has the ability to transform your
relationships and your life.

Connecting with that vibration and holding
your attention there is a skill that will
serve you better than any
act your can perform.

Bringing you heart into resonance
with the rhythm of the Universe
will balance you in magical ways.

LOVE

3

"If you feel a sense of Divine Impersonal Love toward everyone, no one could hurt you."

Emmet Fox

Attachment is what causes suffering.

Holding Divine Love allows us to see
beyond behavior of others
and separates the ego aspects of love.

When Love ceases to be "personal"
it allows compassion to flow.
Divine Love is the essence of God,
the light within our hearts.

We are all emissaries for this amazing,
healing, and powerful gift.

LOVE 4

"To realize God as Love is
the remedy for fear -- and the
only real one."

Emmet Fox

LOVE 4

Realizing fear is one way to get rid of it
— but that is focusing on the fear.

The way out of fear is to embrace Love;
Divine Love and
know it as your Truth.

Love has the power to heal.

Hold love in your heart and soul
and claim it fully. Then, fear has
no place in your life.

LOVE 5

"Divine Love never fails,
it must be in your own heart
and cannot operate from
outside. . ."

Emmet Fox

LOVE 5

Accepting and owning Love
within is knowing God.

The ever present Oneness that animates
all life is yours.
It is the essence of your being.
You are not lovable, you are Love.
Taking time to embrace and connect
with this Divine Love
from within will empower you!

Stop looking for someone to love you
and step into our
own Divine essence.

You are Love.
The love you seek is already yours.

LOVE 6

"The only place where Divine Love can exist, as far as you are concerned is in your own heart. Any love that is not in your heart does not exist for you, and therefore cannot of course help you in any way."

~ Emmet Fox

LOVE 6

Divine Love
is not something outside yourself
that you must find.
It is within, and you must open yourself
and your heart to allow it to express.

When you let go of attachments to fear,
anger, resentment, material things,
relationships, etcetera, you open your
heart and allow Love to flow.

It is part of your innate Divinity.

You need not seek love.
It is your very essence.

LOVE 7

"When you love God more
than you love your problems,
you will be healed."

~Emmet Fox

LOVE 7

Having a problem is fear in action.
"Where there is fear, there cannot be love."
Emmet Fox.

Letting go of fear and connecting with
Divine Love and fully
owning it will heal you.

Changing your focus from "the problem"
to a focus on LOVE
is a shift of consciousness.

Step into Love —claim it, think about it
and practice it.

Use the Law of Principle and
Intelligence too!

Great for LOVE

When you are feeling fearful,
treat for Love.

When you are seeking something
outside yourself to make you happy,
treat for Love.

When you are feeling alone, lonely,
isolated, fearful, anxious, or
your self confidence is low,
treat for Love

Love is the essence of your being.
Reconnecting by using prayer or
meditating on Love will
bring you back into
alignment with your Truth.

LOVE Treatment

God is Love.

What God is, I am.

Knowing that, I can accept that
the essense of me is LOVE.
I open my heart and allow Love
to flow from and through me.
I am filled with the light of love
and Iam blessed.

And so it is!

Aspect Four

God is

INTELLIGENCE

Intelligence I

"When you clearly realize that this is an intelligent Universe it will make a major difference in your life."

— Emmet Fox

INTELLIGENCE 1

God is Intelligence.

The universe is not lacking nor does it
have any unnecessary aspects.
It is harmony.

The laws of the Universe, when accepted,
allow all intelligence to flow for the
greatest good.
It is always available and unwavering.

Open to this wisdom.

Intelligence 2

"God has every quality of personality except its limitations."

~ Emmet Fox

INTELLIGENCE 2

The human mind cannot imagine a personality
that is not limited.
That is part of the "forgetting" of our
spiritual nature.

However, whether the human mind
can conceptualize or not, does not matter.

Recognize this is an Intelligent Universe.

When you connect with your spiritual nature
and own this as yours,
life will transform.

All ideas work for the common good.
Harmony!
There are no missing or extra parts.

Intelligence 3

"It is obvious that in an intelligent Universe there cannot be any disharmony because all ideas must work together for the common good."

— Emmet Fox

INTELLIGENCE 3

Aligning with Divine Intelligence
will open up possibilities and provide
insights previously unknown.

Acknowledging God is Intelligence
will allow you to move beyond
"belief" based reality into a
new dimension of wisdom.

A connection that is limitless!

Intelligence 4

"... there can be no clashing or overlapping anywhere, and neither can there be lack."

Emmet Fox

When you recognize God is Intelligence
you see perfection.
There is nothing missing, no excess,
no lack — there is order in the intelligence.

That is the basis of the Universe -
the intelligence that is the organizing
factor of all that is.

Surrender to this aspect and allow this
intelligence to flow to and
through you into
your life and beyond.

Intelligence 5

"God is not merely intelligent,
but God is Intelligence itself."

Emmet Fox

INTELLIGENCE 5

There is an expansiveness in understanding
God is Intelligence.

What God is, we are.
Every aspect of God is an aspect we process.
Claiming this aspect opens us to a bounty
of wisdom that is unlimited.

Knowing that, in times of indecision and
confusion, all we have to do is get quiet
and connect with this infinite mind.

This is our Source
and our birthright as an
expression of the Divine.

Intelligence   6

"...when people outgrow the
childish idea that God is
just a magnified man, they go
to the opposite extreme and
think of God as merely a blind
force, like gravity or electricity."

~ Emmet Fox

INTELLIGENCE 6

The aspect of God is Intelligence is powerful
beyond our imagination.

Developing a more mature idea
of God opens us to a wisdom
and flow of knowledge
that can transform our lives.

Recognizing this and connecting with
this Divine Intelligence is a process
of maturity.

It requires us to surrender into the
unknown. It is through this surrender
that we allow new ideas
and information to come to us.

Intelligence 7

"You should treat yourself for Intelligence at least two or three times a week, by thinking about it and claiming it for yourself."

— Emmet Fox

INTELLIGENCE 7

When you treat for Intelligence you are
growing and developing this
aspect within yourself.

You are connecting with this "bigger"
knowing and open yourself to being led,
guided, and opening your intuition
to this power.

Let your thinking mind rest,
and allow your higher self to connect.

Treat for
INTELLIGENCE

Treat for Intelligence to open your mind
to the possibilities.

Let your ego go, and surrender to the Divine
Mind. It is through an open mind, heart and
a knowing of your innate Truth that you can
make contact with this magnificent portal.

You can become a channel for this
intelligence and it can transform any
situation.

Quiet your mind and let go of the outcome.
You will be led.

Intelligence
Treatment

There is one Universal power
and that is the source of all life.

I am an expression of that power in
physical form.

I open myself to Divine Mind and the
innate intelligence it encompasses. This
wisdom is limitless and expands my
mind to all possibilities .

It is a blessing to accept and
understand this aspect of God. I give
thanks for this gift.

And so it is.

Aspect Five

God is

SOUL

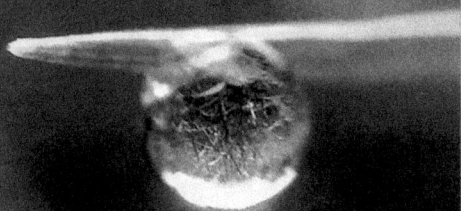

SOUL   I

"Soul is the aspect of God
by virtue of which it is able to
"individualize" itself."

                    ~ Emmet Fox

SOUL 1

The Oneness, Source, God
individualizes itself into
human form within each of us.

Soul is our Divine spark — the light within—
our unique expression of God.

God can individualize into an infinite
number of unique being.
A perfect one-of-a-kind
unit of consciousness.
But, yet all still part of the Oneness.

SOUL 2

"You are the presence of God
at the point you are."

~ Emmet Fox

SOUL 2

We can be compared to a light bulb
The electric current is always there,
but the bulb must be
turned on to glow.

When we raise our consciousness,
we glow.

We are connecting with our Divinity.

The "electricity" is always there,
we just have to awaken.

SOUL   3

"God individualizes as
(hu)man, and so you are really
an individualization of God."

— Emmet Fox

SOUL. 3

We are all the individualization
of the Oneness, Source, Creator,
God.

We are a unique expression,
a one-of-a-kind embodiment,
experiencing the three
dimensional world of the senses.

SOUL   4

> " . . . man cannot be separated
> from God in reality,
> but he can be separated
> in human belief."
>
>   ~ Emmet Fox

SOUL. 4

The light of the Divine within can
never be extinguished.

The degree to which it shines is a
matter of personal consciousness.
When you are aware of your Truth
(that you are an expression of the Divine
in human form)
then your light shines and
your world is filled with joy.

However, if your belief is one of separation,
then you experience fear, pain, and struggle.
This is what Eckhart Tolle
calls the "pain body."

SOUL 5

"...ancient Egyptians spoke
of man as a beam of the
sun... This is a wonderful
idea and expresses
the truth beautifully."

~ Emmet Fox

SOUL. 5

God is Soul.

We are an individualization —a ray of the sun,
not divided.

Recognizing this and allowing it to express
from within you,
will transform your life.

Thinking of yourself as a ray of the sun
means you are all aspects if the sun —
individualized as a ray.

What God is — you are!

SOUL 6

"The word 'individual' means undivided. Most people seem to think it suggests separateness, but actually individual means undivided, and God has the power of individualizing itself without, so to speak, breaking himself into parts."

~ Emmet Fox

SOUL. 6

Soul is the wholeness of the Source
within the vastness and abundance of
all nature.

God can never be depleted.

As a unique expression (ray) of the Divine,
we each poses every aspect of God,
fully and completely.

This is the Soul of who we are.

SOUL

7

"… Divine Mind becomes
self-conscious in you."

Emmet Fox

SOUL. 7

Soul is the essence of God within.

Without human expression there is no
outlet for Divine action.

God is Soul
provides a means for God to show up
in physical form and express
the uniqueness of you.

You are what God is doing today!

Treat for SOUL

God is Soul.

Treat for this when you are feeling a sense of separation and confusion.

Treat for Soul when you are too caught up in your ego mind and the pulls from the 3-D material world.

Remembering your Divine nature will allow you to surrender into the present moment.

Get present and open up into the deep understanding of your own Divine perfection.

SOUL Treatment

God is Soul.

I am the individualization of God and that essence is my Soul.

With that understanding I accept and embody my Divinity with Joy and Purpose. Knowing this is so, I live fully and wholly in the spiritual abundance that is my birthright.

I am filled with gratitude for this understanding and embrace it totally.

I release this into the One Mind and know it is so!

Aspect Six

God is

SPIRIT

SPIRIT   I

"Spirit cannot deteriorate.
It is the opposite of matter.
Matter is always
deteriorating."

~ Emmet Fox

SPIRIT. 1

There is a light inside that cannot be
extinguished, even if ignored or
unacknowledged.
It is the essence and core of "being".
It is the spirit, the spark,
that animates life.

Furthermore, it doesn't end in
human death.
It is released —the wave dissolves
back into the ocean.
It returns to the great ONENESS
that has no beginning and no end.

SPIRIT   2

"You are Spirit.
Spirit cannot die and
was never born."

~ Emmet Fox

SPIRIT. 2

Spirit is the essence of God within.

Spirit animates the physical and has all
the aspects of God.

It is the invisible force that sustains
life, that breathes us.

It cannot be observed, weighed, or
measured.
It is the foundation of our life
experience —but never seen.

SPIRIT   3

"You are eternal,
divine, unchanging
spirit in your true nature."

~ Emmet Fox

SPIRIꞬ. 3

As soon as we take form (being born) we
forget that we are Spirit.
We grow up thinking that what we see and
experience with our senses is the only reality.

It is the reality created by our human
experience — an illusion.
The illusion becomes real, we know it as our
material world.
However, we are more than that, and the
world is more, as well.
We are Spirit experiencing being human.

Awakening is the process of seeing beyond
the illusion and into the
Truth of our true nature.

"The so called inanimate
objects are really spiritual
ideas. A table, a chair. . .etc.,
are all spiritual ideas seen in
the limited way we
call matter."

~ Emmet Fox

SPIRIG. 4

Understanding this difference is the
key to the Law of Bring.
Once you recognize this Truth,
you can call upon these aspects of God
(yourself) and use them to be the creator
of your own world.

It is your Divine birthright.
There is no need to fear it or question its
validity — just open to it.

Experience the mystery and allow your
creative process to flow.

SPIRIT 5

"Well, Spirit is that which
cannot be destroyed or
damaged or hurt, or
degraded or soiled in anyway.
Spirit cannot deteriorate."

~ Emmet Fox

SPIRIT. 5

This little light of mine,
I'm going to let it shine.

A great song, and so true.
We each are a Spirit having a
human experience.
It is our essence.

Our body is the "matter" that allows us
to navigate our human experience.
Our mind is our playground, and our
emotions provide us the distraction
that assists in the separation that
causes us to forget we are Spirit in
human form.

Never-the-less, we are Spirit.

Awakening is the remembering.

SPIRIT 6

"When something is giving
trouble, affirm and try to
realize that in reality it is
a spiritual idea --and watch
what happens."

~Emmet Fox

SPIRIT. 6

Every physical object was, at first,
an idea in the mind of a person (a
spiritual being).
This is spirit in action—the act of
creation — a spiritual idea.

When you look at things this way, it
can change how it functions — and
how you use it.

Never underestimate the power of
creation, or how recognizing some
"thing" as a spiritual idea can alter
your relationship with it

SPIRIT 7

"The thinner the veil of matter the more beauty do we see, and the thicker the veil of matter the less beauty we see."

—Emmet Fox

The veil of matter is the limitations
created by our thoughts.
The more dense matter appears in
our lives, the more we are attached
to our physical existence and less to
our spiritual nature.

We get bogged down in old
thought patterns of the past and
worry of the future.
We forget that our essence is our
Spiritual Nature.

We connect with the aspect of God
is Spirit, we open ourselves to the
joy of being and more beauty
abounds.

Treat for SPIRIT

God is Spirit.

When you are feeling stuck and a bit hopeless
treat for Spirit.

If you forget that your are connected to the
Divine Intelligence and that every act is an act
of Creation, then treat for Spirit.

If you need to remember that you are a Spirit
having a human experience, then treat for
Spirit.

Surrender to your Higher Self and your
innate knowing.

SPIRIT Treatment

God is the light that animates life.

I am animated by this light.

I accept that I am an expression of God walking on the earth. Living and experiencing life as a human being. I embody all aspects of God fully and completely. I allow Spirit to move through me, as me.

I am so grateful for knowing that there is a spiritual idea within everything and everyone, including me, and all my creative pursuits. It is unlimited.

I claim this, in all its fullness..

Aspect Seven

God is

PRINCIPLE

Principle I

"Whatever comes to you, whatever happens to you, whatever surrounds you, will be in accordance with your consciousness, and nothing else; that whatever is in your consciousness must happen no matter who tires to stop it; whatever is NOT in your consciousness cannot happen"

~ Emmet Fox

PRINCIPLE. 1

Understanding God is Principle is seeing that there is a "nuts and bolts" dynamic in our spiritual nature.

There are Spiritual Laws that governs our human experience. Our consciousness is the center of our mastery.

Nothing can or will exist in our human experience without having the consciousness that matches the experience we seek. That is the law.

Elevating your consciousness is a process of awakening. It requires the ability to let go and surrender into all the aspects.

Principle 2

"God is Principle, the principle of perfect harmony, and therefore perfect harmony is the Law of Being."

~ Emmet Fox

PRINCIPLE. 2

The Law of Bring is understanding
that Divine Principle is the only
power that exists.

Learning to tune into it will bring the
harmony and flow of God (Life)
in your experiences.

The magic of prayers being answered.
It is not magic, it is Principle!

Principle 3

"... things will melt away under the realization that Divine Principle is the only power that exists..."

~ Emmet Fox

PRINCIPLE. 3

Understanding Divine Principle
(perfect harmony) and tuning into it
will transform your experience.

Trying to fight principle —for
example, not accepting gravity, is
futile.
Accepting it and working with it will
realize ease and harmony.

When you are fighting or resisting,
you are not in sync with
Divine Principle.

Principle 4

105.1 MHz

108.0

3

"... tune in with Divine
Principle, and then we
find things coming right."

~ Emmet Fox

PRINCIPLE. 4

Divine Principle recognizes that our
connection to Source is not hit or miss
—it is consistent.

What is hit or miss is our alignment with
the principle.
The example of the radio station makes it
clear. If you want to listen to a Jazz station,
you don't tune into a Country station and
wonder why you'er not hearing Jazz!

Align with Source through prayer
(Spiritual mind treatment) and watch
synchronicities begin to flow into your life.

Principle 5

"God is principle. These principles were true a billion years ago and they will be true a billion years hence."

~ Emmet Fox

PRINCIPLE. 5

There are Universal principles that have
always been and will always be — like
"water seeks its own level".
These are Laws of Nature.

When we align with these principles we
come into harmony with God and life
flows with ease.

Resistance or denial only serves to create
disharmony and suffering.

Principle 6

"We have problems and troubles because we have tuned out mentally from God."

~ Emmet Fox

PRINCIPLE. 6

When we are suffering or life becomes
difficult we often turn to God to seek help.
What we need to do is realign ourselves
with Divine Principle.

God is Principle is a knowing, a level of
consciousness that is elevated beyond our
ego yearning and material desires.

Surrender to this understanding and there,
the flow of ease exists.

Principle   7

"Scientific prayer does not try to change the Law . . . It does not ask God to change the laws of nature for our convenience, but it tunes us in . . . "

Emmet Fox

PRINCIPLE. 7

When we accept the ideas of the Law
of Nature and align our mind with the
Mind of God, then our lives bloom.

This is understanding
God is Principle.
It is consistent and ever present.

As we awaken to this understanding
the more good show us in our lives.

Treat for PRINCIPLE

God is Principle.

When you feeling out of sync and things are just not going right, treat for Principle.

When you want to raise your consciousness and align with your true nature.

When you question how things work and find yourself clinging to old ways of navigating the world.

Or, as a reminder that the power of nature is God, and you are an expression of God - treat for Principle.

PRINCIPLE Treatment

God is everywhere and in everything.

I am an expression of God in
human form.

I accept and embody my good,
understanding that the laws of nature
are true for me. God is the Principle
that runs through life and through me.
It is true today as it was and always
will be.

I am blessed by this knowing and
surrender to its powerful presence, in
me and all things.
And, so it is.

*"Who looks outside dreams.
Who looks inside awakens."*

- Carl Jung

www.ingramcontent.com/pod-product-compliance
Lightning Source LLC
LaVergne TN
LVHW051413080426
835508LV00022B/3063